SPORTS FROM COAST TO COAST™

VOLLEYBALL

RULES, TIPS, STRATEGY, AND SAFETY

— SANDRA GIDDENS AND OWEN GIDDENS —

rosen
central™

The Rosen Publishing Group, Inc.,
New York

Published in 2005 by The Rosen Publishing Group, Inc.
29 East 21st Street, New York, NY 10010

First Edition

Library of Congress Cataloging-in-Publication Data

Giddens, Sandra.
Volleyball: rules, tips, strategy, and safety / Sandra Giddens and Owen Giddens.
p. cm.—(Sports from coast to coast) Includes bibliographical references and index. ISBN 1-4042-0185-8 (library binding)
1. Volleyball—Juvenile literature. [1. Volleyball.]
I. Giddens, Owen. II. Title. III. Series.

GV1015.34.G53 2004
796.325—dc22

2003024887

Manufactured in the United States of America

CONTENTS

Chapter One History of Volleyball   4

Chapter Two Playing the Game   10

Chapter Three Training and Conditioning   22

Chapter Four Striving for Gold   30

Glossary   39

For More Information   41

For Further Reading   43

Bibliography   45

Index   46

CHAPTER ONE

History of Volleyball

Not many people know that volleyball originated in the United States. The founder of the game was a man by the name of William G. Morgan, born in 1870, in a town called Lockport in upstate New York. In 1895, he became the director of physical education for the Young Men's Christian Association (YMCA), in Holyoke, Massachusetts. The YMCA had been founded in London, England, in 1844. It was created by businessmen who saw young men going overboard with their drinking and gambling habits and wanted them to live more productive lives. At the YMCA, the game of basketball was the most popular game at the time, but

Here, opposing teams collide at the net. Although volleyball originated in the United States, it has only recently become as popular there as it has around the world.

Morgan, who was in charge of designing physical programs for all ages, felt that he needed another game for the more mature players. He soon invented a game that he named mintonette. The name of the game would later be changed to volleyball.

Morgan felt that basketball, invented in 1891 by his friend James A. Naismith, was just too exhausting for older players. From the game of tennis, he discarded the rackets and raised the height of the net. He then asked the Spalding Manufacturing Company to devise a new type of ball, lighter and more responsive than the basketball. In 1896, he arranged the first volleyball exhibition game at Springfield College between local firefighters and city employees. The game was first described in the July 1896 issue of the magazine *Physical Education.*

The game was a combination of basketball, baseball, handball, and tennis. The net was six feet, six inches high, and a varying number of players were on either side of the net. There were not many rules at first and the ball could be hit many times before it sailed over the net again. The game was nine innings long, like baseball. Each team served three times each inning. The object of the game was to keep the ball in play over the net. If the ball hit the net, it was considered a foul. Today the object of the game is to hit the ball, within bounds, to the ground, so the opposing team cannot return it.

This is a photograph of William G. Morgan, the man who invented volleyball.

These players gear up for a friendly game at a YMCA in St. Louis, Missouri, in the early twentieth century.

Over 100 Years of Volleyball

1895 William G. Morgan creates the game of mintonette, later named volleyball.

1896 The first volleyball team, Holyoke YMCA, is formed.

1900 Volleyball comes to Canada.

1905 Volleyball comes to Cuba.

1908 Volleyball comes to Japan.

1910 Volleyball comes to China and the Philippines.

1914 Armed forces start playing volleyball.

1916 Filipino players develop the spike.

1928 The U.S. Volleyball Association is founded.

1930 The first two-man beach volleyball game is played in California.

1947 Egypt is the first Arab and African country to organize volleyball activities.

1948 First European Championship held in Rome; Czechoslovakia wins.

1949 The first men's Volleyball World Championship.

Teams from China and the Philippines face off in an outdoor game in 1915.

This player from Manila, Philippines, spikes a ball over the net in a game in the early twentieth century.

1964 The first Olympic volleyball tournaments are played in Tokyo; the men's gold medal goes to the USSR and the women's gold goes to Japan.

1973 The first women's World Cup is played in Uruguay; the USSR wins.

1983 The Association of Volleyball Professionals (AVP) is formed.

1984 The United States wins the men's Olympic gold in Los Angeles.

1987 First Beach Volleyball World Championship is played in Ipanema, Brazil.

1988 The U.S. men's team wins its second Olympic gold medal in Seoul, South Korea.

1995 Volleyball is 100 years old; Morgan Trophy is created.

1996 The first Olympic Beach Volleyball Games are held in Atlanta, Georgia. The men's gold goes to the United States. The women's gold goes to Brazil.

2004 Beach volleyball gets its own Olympic stadium in Athens, Greece.

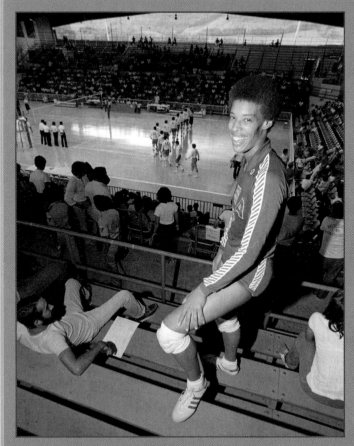

A member of the 1979 U.S. Olympic women's Volleyball Squad takes a break. The 1979 Olympics were held in Moscow, Russia.

While stationed in Tunisia, U.S. soldiers from the 57th Fighter Group play a volleyball match. Since 1914, U.S. Armed Forces have played volleyball to keep their energy and spirits up.

Interest in the game of volleyball quickly spread throughout the United States and the rest of the world, largely because of the global reach of the YMCA. In 1905, the game was introduced in Cuba. In 1908, it was introduced in Tokyo, and in 1910, China and the Philippines were exposed to this new sport. Filipino players soon developed a new technique in which they hit the ball very high so that another person on their team could position himself to smack the ball down hard on the other side. The set and spike were born! The Filipinos called the technique the *bomba* or "kill," and the player who made the shot was called the *bomberino*.

Volleyball soon became a popular sport with American soldiers. In fact, during World War I (1914–1917), volleyball became part of the official training program at military camps around the world. In 1916, volleyball was added to many school and college physical education programs. In 1922, the first YMCA-sponsored volleyball championships were held in Brooklyn, New York, with twenty-seven participating teams from eleven states. In 1928, the United States Volleyball Association was formed. In 1949, the first Volleyball World Championships were held in Prague,

Czechoslovakia. In 1957, the International Olympic Committee designated volleyball as an Olympic team sport, and the first Olympic competition was held at the Tokyo games in 1964. Today, there are more than 200 national federations in the Fédération Internationale de Volleyball (FIVB), based in Paris, and an estimated 800 million people play this fun sport at least once a week.

In 1942, William G. Morgan died, never knowing that the game he had created would one day be so popular throughout the world and become a thrilling Olympic sport. In 1995, 100 years after the invention of the game, the Morgan Trophy was established to honor the best male and female college volleyball players in the United States.

CHAPTER TWO

Playing the Game

This player returns a volley during a game of beach volleyball.

Volleyball can be played most everywhere. You can find it played in schools, recreation centers, playgrounds, and even on the beach. It can be played at any time of the year, both day and night (of course with lights!). Boys and girls of all ages enjoy playing the sport. There are men and women over the age of sixty-five who are still active in playing volleyball. All you really need for an informal game is a net, a ball, a court, and yes, you need the players. Most players wear lightweight clothes like T-shirts and shorts. In beach volleyball, women wear two-piece outfits almost like bikinis.

Beach volleyball evolved from the popular social games

of volleyball played on many beaches around the world. It is played on sand courts that can be formed either naturally or built specifically for this purpose. Instead of a team of six players, each team in beach volleyball consists of two players. It is one of the few sports where female competitors earn more, on average, than males.

In the indoor game, each side consists of six players. The actual volleyball court is rectangular in shape, 29 feet, 6 inches wide and 59 feet long (9 by 18 meters). The net (usually more than 7 feet in height), is set up across the width of the court and divides the court into two halves. The net is 32.8 feet (10 m) long and 3.3 feet (1 m) wide and is made of black or dark brown mesh string. Poles holding the net are equipped with antennae that extend beyond the height of the net, creating a foul-line marker. The court is also divided by lines. The centerline is directly under the net. There are also lines on each side of the court, parallel to the net and 10 feet (3 m) away. These lines are the attack lines. The side-lines indicate out of bounds, and the endline, which also indicates out of bounds, is the line the server stands behind when serving the ball. The ball, when inflated, weighs approximately 9 or 10 ounces (255 to 283 grams) and its circumference (the distance around it) is approximately 26 inches (63.5 to 68.6 centimeters). It is smaller than a basketball and much bigger than a baseball.

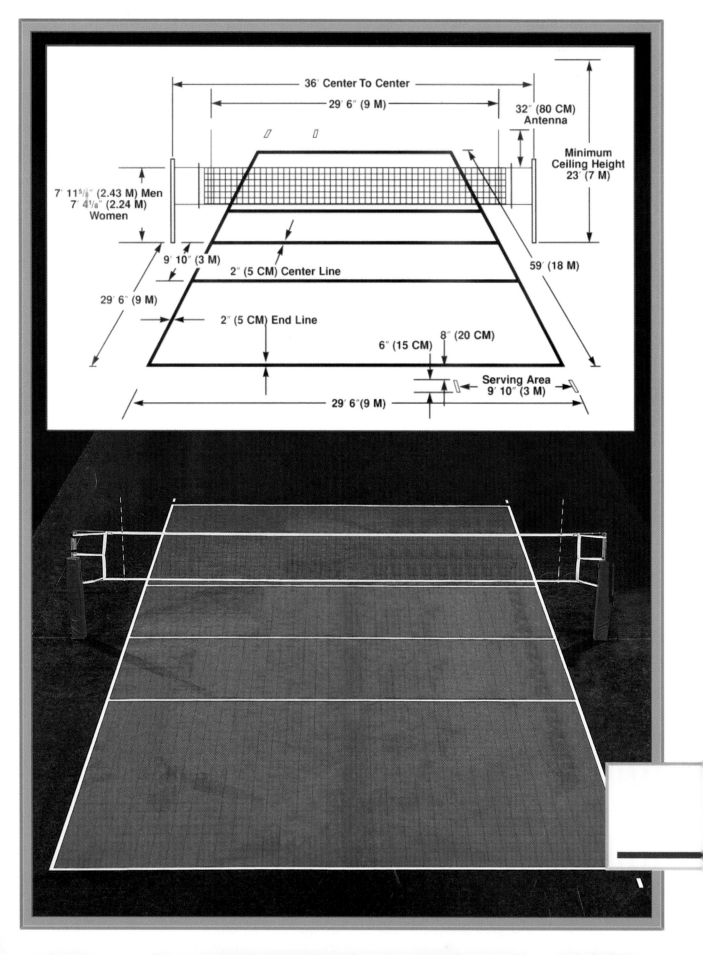

The officials in competitive volleyball include a referee, a scorer, an umpire, and line judges.

Volleyball is a game of nonstop motion. The ball is continuously in play. Players can tap the ball, pass it, or hit it. By hitting the ball back and forth over the net with the hands, forearms, head, or any part of the body, play is continued until one team fails to keep the ball in the air or until a rule violation is committed. Players are not allowed to catch the ball or hit the ball twice in a row. A team is allowed to hit the ball three times in addition to the block before it must be returned across the net. At all times a team tries to prevent the ball from hitting the ground in their area. In a six-person volleyball team, three players stand near the front of the net, in front of the attack line, and the other three are back-row players or defenders. Any player can pass or set up the ball, but it is only those in the front row who can block or spike the ball. The server stands behind the endline when he or she serves the ball over the net. The ball is tossed into the air and the server strikes it with an open hand or fist. Only one attempt is allowed on the serve. The server keeps serving as long as his or her team continues to win points. Points are scored by successfully landing the ball in the court of the opponents without it being returned. The serve must rotate to a new player on the team each time the team wins back the serve.

Before the 1990s, only the serving team could score points in a volleyball game. This means that if the ball hits the ground on the opposing team's side, play stops and the serving team scores the point.

Although amateur volleyball can be played anywhere there are two people, a ball, and a net, professional volleyball requires a regulation-size court. A regulation-size volleyball court measures 29.6 feet (9 m) by 59 feet (18 m).

Indoor Volleyball Rules

Players

- Six players on each team can play on the court at one time.
- Players cannot touch the net.
- Players cannot cross the centerline.
- The ball is still in play if it touches any part of the sideline or endline.

Service

- A rally begins with a serve from a player behind the endline. The serve must go over the net but can touch the net as long as it goes into the opponent's court.
- On the serve, if the ball does not go over net or goes out of bounds, service is lost.
- No second service attempt is permitted.

Ball Contact

- A team is allowed to make ball contact three times before clearing the ball over the net.
- A player cannot make contact with the ball with two consecutive touches.
- If a player blocks the ball and the ball continues into his or her court, the team is allowed three touches. A block at net does not count as a touch.

Rally Ends When

- A team touches the ball more than three times before clearing the ball over the net.
- The ball does not go over the net.
- The ball hits the ground.
- The ball goes out of bounds.
- The ball hits the ceiling or any object above the court.

This also means the server can serve again. But if the ball hits the ground on the serving side, the play is stopped and the opposing team serves. No point is awarded, because, to repeat, only the serving team can score the point. Before the ball is served, the team rotates, moving clockwise one position, and the person in the back right position becomes the new server. When a hitter on the serving team hits the ball out of bounds, the receiving team does not get the point but gets the chance to serve. If a player on the receiving team touches the ball before it goes out of bounds, the serving team gets the point.

As mentioned, until very recently, a point could only be scored by the serving team. If the team failed to win the point, the serve went back to the opposing team. This was called a side-out. This rule was changed in the late 1990s to increase the attraction of the game. In rally scoring a point is scored in each serve. Rally scoring is used in the deciding game of a match and in international volleyball competitions. Beach volleyball is usually one game, using side-out scoring, or best out of three using rally scoring. In a traditional game, the first team to score 15 points wins. In rally scoring it is 25 points. Usually, a game is over when one team scores 15 points, but the winning team has to succeed by a two-point spread. So a 15 to 14 game, for example, would continue until it became a two-point spread of 16 to 14. A match is a series of games, and to win a match a team must win two out of three or three out of five games.

If this all sounds a little complicated, just imagine following the ball from your team's side: The server would take hold of it, go behind the endline, and toss it up in the air, striking it so it rises above the net to the opposing team. If it is out of bounds, then the opposing team has to serve it back. If the ball hits the ground on the opposing side, a point is scored for your team. If the ball is touched by a player on the opposing team, the players will try to set up their team by passing the ball toward the net and smacking it down over the net on the other side so they can start winning points when they serve.

Mechanics of the Game

The two most common types of serves are the overhand and the underhand serve. In the underhand serve, the ball is held in one hand, and the other hand swings and hits below and behind the ball. In the overhead serve, the ball is tossed into the air a little bit in front of the server's head. The other hand is pulled back and swung forward to hit the volleyball. Servers start the volley and get one attempt to hit the ball over the net. It is essential to have accurate serves. The server can also have many styles of serving, just like pitching in baseball. The server can hit a ball with topspin, or serve a fast ball, or serve a deceptive floater that seems to wobble and slip uncertainly in the air.

It is very important for a team to work together to set up passes so the last person to touch the ball makes a strong and accurate hit at the opposing team. A bump pass or forearm pass is when your arms are extended out straight with your hands locked with thumbs together. The ball hits the arms between the wrist and elbow. The overhead pass is when the arms are over the head and the knees are bent. The fingers are extended after releasing the ball. The bump pass is used if the team is receiving a serve or if the opposing team has hit the ball with power.

A set is the process of moving the ball from player to player until it is positioned properly for the final hitter to put it over the net effectively. The player passes the ball to his or her teammate, who sets or guides the ball to the hitter. The hitter, of course, tries to win the point

This volleyball player drops to her knees to make a save. Volleyball players wear kneepads because they frequently have to dive for the ball.

These front row players rise up to block a spike from the opposition. It is important to play good defense if you want your team to win.

This player rises above the net to spike the ball back to the opposing team. Spiking the ball is an effective way to score.

by smacking the ball over the net. The setter has to anticipate the movement of his or her teammates, as well as appreciate the strengths and weaknesses of the opposing players, so that the ball is placed where the final hitter can score a point.

The Spike

The spike! It is one of the most dramatic and dynamic single movements in all of sports. The sheer beauty and athleticism of a well-executed spike can take one's breath away. It is the home run, the slam dunk, the touch-down, the slap-shot goal, and the 300-yard drive of volleyball.

—Brad Saindon, head volleyball coach, Arizona State University

Spiking is very exciting to watch. It is a powerful smash over the net. It is when the hitter slams the ball over the net and down on the opponent's side of the court. To spike the ball, the player must jump very high in the air, using perfect timing, and hit the ball powerfully, placing it so it is extremely difficult to return. The opposite of the spike is the tip. This is a lightly hit ball deflected or dropped into the opponent's court and is used by the spiker to surprise opposing blockers when they anticipate a spike.

As important as it is to set the ball up to either win a point or get the ball back to your side of the net, team defense is just as important.

Players need to have fast reflexes when they are playing close to the net. If this player misses the block, the rest of he team will have to try to make the save. A good defender doesn't let pressure distract him or her from doing the job.

It is vital that the players prevent the spiker from the opposing team from getting the ball on their side of the court. At all times, the defense must be alert, anticipating and watching. They have to move along the net to the spot where they think the ball will be hit. The player opposite the spiker then has to jump up very high with fingers spread wide and block the ball. If the block is successful, the ball will fall back on the opponent's side, never reaching its anticipated goal. There are times the ball gets by the blocker, though. The rest of the team has to be on guard to handle the ball when this happens and defend their side. The members of the team get down very low to the ground by bending their legs. They stay low to the ground so they can dive for the ball. Sometimes the defensive player gets down so low to the ground that his or her body is stretched parallel to the floor. This movement is called a dig. Digs and other successful defensive moves are the most difficult shots and therefore they are called saves.

It is true that a good defensive play can literally save the game and be a major contribution toward winning.

A good defensive team will be able to wear down and frustrate the opponent, forcing attack errors. Generally the better defensive team will win close matches.

—Jim Stone, head volleyball coach, Ohio State University

Beach Volleyball

The rules for beach volleyball are somewhat different from those of indoor volleyball. Beach volleyball is played by two teams of two

This beach volleyball player sets the ball so his teammate can spike it. Good teamwork is necessary for beach volleyball. Although the playing area is smaller and the ball is bigger, beach volleyball takes just as much skill as indoor volleyball.

members each. In place of player rotation, the players alternate serves. The ball used for the outdoor game happens to be a little larger than the one for the indoor game as well as a little less inflated. The net is also elevated to 8 feet (2.4 m). One of the facets of beach volleyball is the use of hand signals by players to indicate to their partner what sort of play they intend to make. These signals are done behind the players' backs.

21

CHAPTER THREE

Training and Conditioning

Drills are like recipes. With the right ingredients and directions, anyone can cook, but it takes a master chef or a master coach to mix and vary ingredients to suit the needs of different individuals.

—Mary Wise, head women's volleyball coach, University of Florida

Volleyball is played in most schools as part of the physical education curriculum. There are many practice drills players can do in order to improve their game. Building up endurance, strength, timing, and coordination are important in the game of volleyball. Running can build endurance and stamina.

It's important to warm up before a practice or a game.

It is also important that players stretch so that they can dive for a ball. Stretching helps in becoming more flexible. Stretching is extremely important for players because the sport puts pressure and strain on body parts, especially below the waist. Doing all that squatting, lunging, and digging can affect the body. Stretching raises your core body temperature and lubricates your joints, preventing injury. Try this stretch: lie down on your back with your head on the ground, one ankle crossed over the opposite bent knee. With your hands behind the bent knee, pull the leg into your middle until you feel a stretch in the back of the thigh. Make sure your head stays down in a relaxed position and increase the pressure only slightly each time you stretch. Reverse legs and ankles. Remember, when you stretch it is important to hold for a count, and do not bounce.

It is necessary for players to be able to jump high in order to block. Jumping also helps in strengthening leg muscles. Such drills as jumping up and down as high as you can and jumping rope are good exercises. It is also essential in volleyball to have strong hands, especially fingers. Such activities like squeezing different sized rubber balls can assist in strengthening the hands. You can also tighten your fist and spread the fingers wide; doing this exercise consecutively allows the hand to become more agile.

Do's, Don'ts, and Practice Ideas

When serving, these are things to do:

- With underhand serves, stand facing the net with the foot opposite the hitting hand forward.

- Hold the ball at waist level.

- Lean forward and swing forward to contact the ball.

- Make sure that the hand holding the ball drops just before contact.

- Hit underneath the ball with the fist or heel of the hand.

- Follow through in the direction of target with your hitting arm.

- With overhand serves, toss the ball 18 inches (46 cm) high, so the ball falls just inside the lead foot in line with your shoulder.

- Keep your elbow and hand at shoulder height or above.

- Shift weight to the lead foot, or step forward as you make contact with the ball.

- Make sure your wrist is firm throughout the serve.

- Contact the ball with the heel of the hand through the middle back of the ball.

- Make sure the contact sound is a thud, not a slap.

- Make sure your hand follows the ball to the target.

- Finish with your hand alongside or within the body line.

This player puts her own unique spin on an overhead serve during a state high school volleyball tournament. Having a good serve is a crucial part of being a good all-around player.

When serving, these are things not to do:

- Don't throw the ball so high you lose control.
- Don't use the foot under your hitting arm.

Practice ideas:

- See how many serves you can do in one minute.
- See how many good serves you can do in a row.
- See how many serves you can hit toward a specific target placed in the opposite court.

When passing, these are things to do:

- Start in the ready position.
- Use straight arms away from the body.
- Keep your knees bent.
- Contact the ball on your forearms.
- Face the direction you want the ball to go and aim the ball toward your target.
- Start out facing the server and always face the ball when you pass.
- Move toward the ball without crossing your feet.
- Try to get to the spot before the ball does.
- With an overhand pass, spread fingers in the shape of the ball over the head.
- Form a triangle with thumbs and pointer fingers; the hands should not be touching.
- Place hands in front of the face close to forehead.
- On contact, set by extending arms and legs.

This player keeps her feet planted and knees bent as she returns a volley from the opposing team. A good player can make the ball go where he or she wants it to go.

When passing, these are things not to do:

- Don't just stand there and do nothing.

- Don't bend your elbows.

- Don't swing your arms too much.

- Don't contact the ball with your hands apart.

- Don't take your eyes off the ball.

- In an overhand pass, don't contact ball with palms of hands.

- In an overhand pass, face away from where ball is coming from.

Practice ideas:

- Three people—a hitter, a passer, and a digger—are all on the same side. The setter faces the passer and the hitter hits a down ball at the passer, who then digs it. The setter then sets the hitter. The drill is continuous and focuses on ball control with all three players.

When hitting, spiking, or blocking, do the following:

- Use approach steps and a two-foot jump.

- Use both arms for swinging forward on takeoff.

This player returns a vicious spike from the opposing team. Having a good defense means the difference between winning and losing in a tight game.

- Snap your wrist for topspin on contact.
- As you leave the floor to jump, pull your hitting arm back with the elbow and hand at shoulder height or higher.
- Have your hand open and relaxed with the palm facing away from the ear.
- Jump up vertically to meet the ball.
- Contact the ball at the peak of the jump with a straight arm.
- Land at least one foot past the contact point.
- Get the ball up the middle of the court so your partner can set it when it is a tough ball in beach volleyball.
- Play the ball low on defense.
- Spread your fingers wide, covering as much space as possible.
- Keep your eye on the ball.

When hitting, spiking, or blocking, don't do the following:

- Don't make a one-foot jump.
- Don't hit the ball with a fist instead of an open hand.

Tipping the ball, as seen here, can be an effective move against unsuspecting defenders. Rather than spiking the ball, the offensive player *(right)* lightly tips the ball over the net.

- Don't swing one hand forward and the other behind.
- Don't use a shot-put arm action.
- Don't close your eyes when blocking.
- Don't close your fingers together when blocking.

Practice ideas:

In pairs, one on each side of the net
- Use the spike to hit across the net.
- Practice jumping before spiking.
- Practice spiking the ball against a wall.

Nowadays visualization is part of most sports training. Players imagine the play before executing it. For example, before serving the ball, the server visualizes where he or she wants it to land. This technique helps a player feel more centered and less anxious. Visualization also helps the player to think positively and enhances his or her ability to concentrate. There are even psychotherapists and coaches who specialize in training athletes to be proficient at visualizations.

CHAPTER FOUR

Striving for Gold

This player dives for the ball during a beach volleyball match at the 1996 Centennial Summer Games.

The Fédération Internationale de Volleyball (FIVB) was founded in 1947, and the world championships were started in 1949. Volleyball was added to the Olympic Games in 1964, and beach volleyball became an Olympic sport in 1996.

As soon as volleyball took off, it was very popular in schools and on the beaches, but it was still a relatively new sport to the Olympics. It was added as a medal sport in 1964 for both men and women. In the early Olympics the dominating volleyball forces were teams from Japan and the Soviet Union (Russia). The Japanese women's team was coached by a man named Hirofumi Daimatsu. Their schedule for practice included training six hours a day, seven days a week, fifty-one weeks a year. Daimatsu was so demanding as a coach, always wanting perfection, that people said he could be verbally and psychologically abusive to his players. He taught the Japanese women new techniques, like a rolling receive, which is when a player dives to the ground, smacks the ball, rolls over, and quickly returns to her feet.

The Soviet Union also became a strong force that other volleyball teams had difficulties beating. The Soviet Union won the first men's Olympic gold medal for volleyball in 1964 and the fighting women's machine of Japan won the women's gold. In 1968, the Soviet Union again won the men's gold as well as the women's gold. In 1972, the Soviet Union's women's team won the gold, and in 1980, both the Soviet Union's men's and women's teams, won the gold in Moscow. The Americans really wanted to compete against the Soviet Union, but the United States boycotted the Moscow games. President Jimmy Carter wanted to protest the former Soviet Union's invasion of Afghanistan and henceforth ordered all the American athletes to stay away from the Moscow Olympics. For the1984 Olympics in Los Angeles, the Soviet Union decided to play tit for tat and boycotted the games. So in 1984, there was a change in the pattern of victories, and the United States' men's volleyball

team won the gold and the United States' women's team won the silver. The 1988 Olympics were held in Seoul, South Korea, and the U.S. teams were finally competing again against the Soviet Union's teams. The Soviet Union's women's team won the gold, but the U.S. men's team, led by such players as Karch Kiraly, Steve Timmons, Dave Saunders, Doug Partie, Jon Root, and Craig Buck, won the Olympic men's gold.

There are many stars in volleyball. One of the most famous spikers in American volleyball history was a woman by the name of Flo Hyman. She was a member of the first group of U.S. women who trained together for the Olympics, beginning in 1974. She and her teammates qualified for the 1980 Olympics, but because of the boycott they were unable to fulfill their dreams. In 1981, she was named the world's best hitter. "The audience would hold its breath when she rose for a spike," said Joan Ackerman-Blount of *Sports Illustrated*. Finally, in the 1984 Olympics in Los Angeles, Hyman and her team, challenged by the Chinese women's team, came in second with the silver. Hyman, who was 6 foot, 5 inches tall (2 m), reported that winning the silver medal was one of the proudest moments of her life! By the end of the 1984 Olympics, Hyman was considered to be the best volleyball player in the world.

After the Olympics, Hyman played in Japan, where she was paid to play the sport she loved, volleyball. In Japan in 1986, while playing a game, Flo Hyman collapsed and died. She was thirty-one

U.S. volleyball team star Karch Kiraly slams the ball back to the opposing team at the 1988 Summer Olympics. Volleyball is popular all around the world among both men and women.

Olympic Indoor Volleyball Results for Gold

Year	Location	Women	Men
1964	Tokyo, Japan	Japan	USSR
1968	Mexico City, Mexico	USSR	USSR
1972	Munich, Germany	USSR	Japan
1976	Montreal, Cananda	Japan	Poland
1980	Moscow, Russia	USSR	USSR
1984	Los Angeles, California	China	USA
1988	Seoul, Korea	USSR	USA
1992	Barcelona, Spain	Cuba	Brazil
1996	Atlanta, Georgia	Cuba	Netherlands
2000	Sydney, Australia	Cuba	Yugoslavia

Team USA plays Team Korea in the Men's Sitting Volleyball quarterfinals at the 2000 Paralympic Games in Sydney, Australia. These players don't let their disabilities get in the way of their enjoyment of volleyball.

years old. She died of a disease named Marfan syndrome, which caused her aorta to rupture. Every year, to commemorate Hyman's achievement and work in support of women's sports, an award is given to a young female athlete from the Women's Sports Foundation. In 1988, she was inducted into the Volleyball Hall of Fame in Holyoke, Massachusetts.

Another great volleyball star, still playing strong, is Karch Kiraly. He is the only volleyball player in Olympic history to win three gold medals. He joined the national team in 1981 and led the U.S. men's volleyball team to two gold medals. He was also named the Most Valuable Player in the 1988 Olympics. Kiraly has an amazing jump serve. He tosses the ball with one hand while his other hand is on his hip. Kiraly was an Olympic winner in indoor volleyball and then went on to play beach volleyball in the 1996 Olympics, where he won his third gold medal. Karch Kiraly has said that "any beach is more attractive than the inside of a stadium . . . you have natural sunlight, girls in bikinis, guys in shorts. What better way to make a living than going to the beach?" Kiraly leads all pro beach volleyball players in career prize money.

Holly McPeak dives for the ball at the 2003 AVP/Nissan Series San Diego Open. Holly McPeak is considered one of the best beach volleyball players in the world.

Some other exciting U.S. stars in beach volleyball are Karolyn Kirby, Holly McPeak, Christopher "Sinjin" Smith, and Kent Steffes. Karolyn Kirby has won more event titles than any other woman on the pro beach circuits. Holly McPeak leads all women in career prize money with more than $1,000,000 in earnings. Christopher Smith is the oldest elite player in the world. He has competed in more beach volleyball events than any other player. And Kent Steffes won the gold medal with Karch Kiraly at the 1996 Atlanta Olympic Games.

In 2004, the Olympics were held in Athens, Greece. The indoor volleyball competition will be held in the Peace and Friendship Stadium, which has a seating capacity of 14,000. The competition will last for more than sixteen days and the men's and women's matches will be held every other day. More than 280 athletes from different countries will participate in the Olympic volleyball championship. Beach volleyball will be at the Olympic Beach Volleyball Center. For the first time in Olympic beach volleyball history, games will take place late in the evenings with lights. The main competition area has a seating capacity of 10,000. Volleyball has come so far from the simple game that William G. Morgan had invented to keep men in shape.

In this photo, the Olympic Beach Volleyball Center is under construction in Athens, Greece, where the 2004 summer Olympics were held. Athens was the home of the first Olympic tournaments.

It is literally played around the world, and even beach volleyball will have its own center in Athens for the 2004 Olympics.

Today there is even a competitive division of volleyball for the disabled. In 1988, the U.S. Congress passed the Olympic and Amateur Sports Act to give equal status to disabled athletes, and the United States Olympic Committee (USOC) has now organized volleyball competitions for athletes in wheelchairs and those with other disabilities.

Junior Olympic volleyball and Junior Olympic beach volleyball are for players eighteen years of age and younger. But U.S. national volleyball competitions are open to players from thirty years of age to seventy-five years of age and over. There are volleyball leagues for players in grade school, junior high, and high school. No matter where you live you can usually find a league for all age groups located close by. You may need to look in the telephone directory to see what is in your area, search the Internet, contact your local YMCA or local recreation center, or ask your school physical education department where the reputable leagues are. Volleyball is being played around the world, and competitions for beach and indoor volleyball exist for players in various skills divisions and age groups. Just as in any other

The U.S. Women's Olympic volleyball team celebrates its third straight victory over the Ukraine during the preliminary competition at the 1996 Olympic Games. Although professional volleyball is demanding and highly competitive, even the pros know that the most important thing about playing volleyball is having a good time.

sport, learning the skills and moves to play volleyball involves time, effort, and commitment. But if you are patient, persistent, and willing to practice a lot, you can become a very good volleyball player, and maybe an Olympic star!

GLOSSARY

ace A serve that scores a point without an opposing player touching the ball.

attack line A line about 10 feet (3 m) from the net.

block When a player jumping in the air uses his or her hands to prevent the ball from passing over the net.

court The area in which a volleyball game is played.

dig A move whereby a player hits a ball from below the waist.

fault An illegal move or play.

forearm pass A hit with straight forearms in front of the body, also called a bump pass.

game point The point that will win the game.

jump serve A serve in which the server tosses the ball and then jumps to hit it.

kill A shot that is impossible for an opponent to return.

match Predetermined number of games.

net ball A ball that touches the net.

overhand serve A serve in which the server tosses the ball and hits it when it is above the head but does not jump to hit it.

pass   To hit the ball to a player on your side with an overhead or a forearm pass.

rally   The time when the ball is in play after being served.

rotation   When a team gets the ball back to serve, players move one position clockwise.

save   To keep the ball from hitting the floor, usually with a dig or dive.

serve   To put the ball in play by hitting it directly over the net and into the other team's court.

set   A high pass from one player to another.

spike   A rapid hit, usually after the ball has been set by another player, that sends the ball hard to the ground.

underhand serve   A serve in which the server tosses the ball and hits it by swinging his or her arm from below the waist.

volley   A series of plays in which the ball is hit back and forth between the two teams.

FOR MORE INFORMATION

Organizations:

USA Volleyball
715 South Circle Drive
Colorado Springs, CO 80910
88-US Volley (888-786-5539)
e-mail: info@usav.org
Web site: http://usavolleyball.org

Disabled Sports/USA Volleyball
451 Hungerford Drive
Suite 100
Rockville, MD 20850
(301) 217-0960
e-mail: information@dsusa.org
Web site: http://dsusa.org

Magazines:

Volleyball Magazine
44 Front Street
Suite 590
Worcester, MA 01608
(800) 437-5828

Web Sites:

Due to the changing nature of Internet links, the Rosen Publishing Group, Inc., has developed an online list of Web sites related to the subject of this book. This site is updated regularly. Please use this link to access the list:

http//:www.rosenlinks.com/scc/voll

FOR FURTHER READING

Beeson, Chris. *Volleyball*. Broomall, PA: Mason Crest Publishers, 2004.

Clemens, Teri. *Get With It, Girls! Life Is Competition*. South Bend, IN: Diamond Communications, 2001.

Crisflied, Deborah. *Winning Volleyball for Girls*. New York: Facts on File, 2002.

Dearing, Joel. *Volleyball Fundamentals*. Champaign, IL: Human Kinetics, 2003.

Ditchfield, Christin. *Volleyball*. New York: Children's Press, 2003.

Jensen, Julie. *Play-by-Play Volleyball*. Minneapolis: Lerner Publications, 2001.

Jordan, Stephanie. *Developing a Successful Girl's and Women's Volleyball Program*. Monterey, CA: Coaches Choice, 2003.

Kiraly, Karch. *Beach Volleyball*. Champaign, IL: Human Kinetics, 1999.

Lucas, Jeff. *Pass, Set, Crush: Volleyball Illustrated*. Wenatchee, WA: Euclid Northwest Publications, 1993.

Manley, Claudia. *Competitive Volleyball for Girls*. New York: Rosen Publishing, 2001.

Martin, Peggy. *101 Volleyball Drills*. Monterey, CA: Coaches Choice, 2002.

Reeser, Jonathan. *Volleyball*. Malden, MA: Blackwell Science, 2002.

Sherrow, Victoria. *Volleyball*. San Diego: Lucent Books, 2002.

Tanner, Mark. *Smarter Volleyball: Principles and Strategies for Winning Doubles*. Kearney, NE: Morris Publishing, 1998.

Viera, Barbara L., and Bonnie Jill Ferguson. *Volleyball: Steps to Success*. Champaign, IL: Human Kinetics, 1996.

BIBLIOGRAPHY

American Sports Education Program. *Coaching Youth Volleyball.* Champaign, IL: Human Kinetics, 2001.

Couvillon, Arthur R. *Sands of Time: The History of Beach Volleyball.* Hermosa Beach, CA: Information Guides, 2002.

Emma, Thomas. *Peak Performance for Volleyball.* Monterey, CA: Coaches Choice, 2003.

Gozansky, Sue. *Volleyball Coach's Survival Guide.* Paramus, NJ: Parker Publishers, 2001.

Scates, Allen E. *Complete Conditioning for Volleyball.* Champaign, IL: Human Kinetics, 2003.

Shondell, Don. *The Volleyball Coaching Bible.* Champaign, IL: Human Kenetics, 2002.

INDEX

B

ball, 5, 8, 10, 11, 13, 15, 16, 18, 20, 21,
        22, 25, 31
baseball, 5, 11, 16
basketball, 4–5, 11
beach volleyball, 10–11, 15, 20–21, 35–36, 37
rules, 20
blocking, 13, 20, 23, 27, 28
bomberino, 8
Buck, Craig, 33

C

Carter, Jimmy, 31
coordination, 22
court(s), 10, 13, 18, 20, 26
    division of, 11
Cuba, 8

D

deciding game, 15
defense, 18, 20
Daimatsu, Hirofumi, 30, 31
dive, 20, 23

F

Fédération Internationale de Volleyball
        (FIVB), 9, 30
foul, 5
foul-line marker, 11

H

handball, 5
hand signals, 21
Hyman, Flo, 33, 35

I

International Olympic Committee, 9
International Volleyball Federation, 9

J

Japan, 30–31, 33
Junior Olympic beach volleyball, 37
Junior Olympic volleyball, 37

K

Kiraly, Karch, 33, 35, 36
Kirby, Karolyn, 36

L

leagues, 37
Lockport, New York, 4
London, England, 4

M

match, 15
McPeak, Holly, 36
mintonette, 5
Morgan, William G., 4–5, 9, 36
Morgan Trophy, 9

N

Naismith, James A., 5
net, 5, 10, 11, 13, 15, 16, 18, 20, 21

O

officials, 13
Olympic and Amateur Sports Act, 37
Olympic Beach Volleyball Center, 36
Olympic Games, 9, 30–31, 33, 35–37

P

Partie, Doug, 33
passes, 16
passing, 13, 16, 26, 27
Philippines, the, 8
Physical Education, 5
players, 10, 13, 15, 16, 18, 20, 21, 23, 31
  blocker, 20
  defensive, 13, 20
  hitter, 15–16, 18, 27
  server, 11, 13, 15, 16, 26
  setter, 18
points, 13, 15, 16, 18
practice drills, 22, 26, 27, 28

R

rally scoring, 15
rolling receive, 31
Root, Jon, 33
rules, 5, 13, 15, 20
  violation of, 13
running, 22

S

Saunders, Dave, 33
serves, 13, 15, 16, 20, 25, 26
  jump serve, 35
  types of, 16
side-out, 15
Smith, Christopher "Sinjin," 36
Soviet Union, 31
Spalding Manufacturing Company, 5
spike, 8, 13, 18

spiker, 18, 20, 33
spiking, 13, 18, 27, 28
Sports Illustrated, 33
Steffes, Kent, 36
strength, 22
stretching, 23

T

teams, 11, 13, 15–16, 20, 30
  opposing, 5, 13, 15–16, 20
  serving, 13, 15
tennis, 5
timing, 22
Timmons, Steve, 33
tip, 18

U

United States, 4, 8–9, 31
United States Olympic Committee (USOC), 37
United States Volleyball Association, 8

V

Volleyball Hall of Fame, 35

W

Women's Sports Foundation, 35
world championships, 8, 30
World War I, 8

Y

Young Men's Christian Association (YMCA),
  4, 8, 37

About the Authors

Dr. Sandra Giddens and Dr. Owen Giddens make their home in Toronto. They have written a number of educational books for Rosen Publishing.

Photo Credits